
GroundTruth AI Advisory
Safeguarding Human Authority in an Algorithmic Age

This work is a human–AI collaboration conducted under human authority, as defined in the Author's Covenant contained in this book. All responsibility for the content rests solely with the human author.

ISBN 978-1-0674754-1-3

First Edition

Dedication

To those who choose responsibility
over permission.

—

Epigraph

"Not everything that can be decided should be."

TABLE OF CONTENTS

Part IV — Institutions Under Pressure

Part V — Misuse, Drift, and Capture

Part VI — The Future of Restraint

Introduction

Why GroundTruth Exists

This book was not written to explain artificial intelligence.

It was written because too many people are allowing artificial intelligence to explain *them*.

Across institutions, governments, faith communities, businesses, and advisory rooms, a quiet shift is taking place. Decisions that were once grounded in human judgment, moral authority, cultural continuity, and lived responsibility are increasingly being reframed as optimization problems. Language is changing. Responsibility is softening. Authority is being redistributed—often without consent, sometimes without awareness.

Artificial intelligence did not create this shift.
But it is accelerating it.

This book exists to draw a line.

The Central Claim

Artificial intelligence can assist human judgment.
It must never replace it.

That distinction sounds obvious. In practice, it is routinely violated.

Not through malice, but through convenience.
Not through coercion, but through reassurance.
Not through rebellion, but through delegation.

Organizations rarely intend to surrender authority. They drift into it—one workflow at a time.

GroundTruth AI Advisory emerged from recognizing that drift early, naming it clearly, and refusing to normalize it.

What GroundTruth Is — and Is Not

GroundTruth is not anti-technology.
It is not nostalgic.
It is not reactionary.
It is not neutral.

GroundTruth is a framework for determining **where artificial intelligence belongs, where it must remain subordinate, and where it must be excluded entirely**.

It begins with a simple premise:

Some decisions are not computational.
Some authority cannot be automated.
Some responsibilities cannot be shared.

When those boundaries are crossed, no amount of efficiency compensates for what is lost.

Why This Book Is a Collaboration

This book is a collaboration between a human author and an artificial intelligence system.

That collaboration is intentional—and constrained.

Artificial intelligence is used here as an analytical instrument: to reflect arguments, surface pressures, model institutional reasoning, and expose optimization bias. It is not used to establish values, determine truth, or arbitrate authority.

The structure of this collaboration mirrors the thesis of the book itself.

The human leads.
The machine assists.
Authority remains non-delegable.

Where the AI appears in the text, it is clearly identified. Where it challenges, that challenge is deliberate. Where it fails to grasp moral, spiritual, or cultural nuance, that failure is instructive.

The form of this book is part of its argument.

Why Authority Matters More Than Accuracy

Modern discourse often treats accuracy as the highest virtue.

It is not.

Accuracy without authority produces compliance, not wisdom.
Efficiency without accountability produces scale, not legitimacy.
Insight without responsibility produces influence, not leadership.

GroundTruth begins from the position that **authority precedes intelligence**, not the other way around. Without a human locus of responsibility—someone who can say *yes*, *no*, or *stop*—intelligence becomes directionless power.

That is not a theoretical risk. It is already visible.

The Domains Where This Matters Most

This book focuses on environments where the cost of misplacing authority is irreversible:

- Faith and spiritual institutions
- Indigenous and sovereign governance
- High-trust advisory and leadership settings
- Correctional, moral, and rehabilitative systems
- Organizations facing existential or cultural decisions

In these domains, the question is not whether AI can help.

The question is whether it should be allowed to lead—even indirectly.

Often, the correct answer is no.

Refusal as Leadership

One of the least discussed skills in the age of artificial intelligence is refusal.

Not reactive refusal.
Not fear-based rejection.
But disciplined, informed, principled refusal.

GroundTruth treats refusal as a core competency.
Exit as an ethical outcome.
Restraint as a leadership signal.

This book will not offer balanced compromises where compromise is inappropriate. It will not pretend that every problem requires a hybrid solution. It will name boundaries and hold them.

That clarity is intentional.

How to Read This Book

This is not a manual.
It is not a product guide.
It is not a sales document.

It is a framework, a warning, and a record.

Some readers will find parts of it uncomfortable.
Some will recognize situations they are already inside.
Some will realize—too late—that they crossed a line without noticing.

If this book helps you decide **not** to deploy AI in a place where it does not belong, it has done its job.

If it helps you reclaim authority you quietly outsourced, it has done more.

A Final Orientation

Artificial intelligence is not the enemy of humanity.

But neither is it neutral.

The future will not be decided by smarter machines.
It will be decided by whether humans remember where judgment must remain human.

GroundTruth exists to make that memory explicit.

The chapters that follow are not suggestions.

They are boundaries.

Author's Covenant

On Human Authority and Artificial Intelligence

This book is a collaboration between a human author and an artificial intelligence system.

It is not a partnership of equals.

This covenant exists to make that distinction explicit, enforceable, and visible to the reader.

---

1. Human Authority Is Non-Delegable

All positions, judgments, refusals, boundaries, and conclusions expressed in this book originate from the human author.

Artificial intelligence does not possess moral agency, lived consequence, spiritual accountability, or institutional responsibility. It therefore cannot hold authority.

Authority, where it appears in this work, remains human and named.

---

2. Artificial Intelligence Is Used Under Constraint

The artificial intelligence participating in this book functions as an analytical instrument only.

It may assist by:

- Organizing ideas
- Stress-testing arguments
- Modeling institutional pressures
- Reflecting common optimization logic

It may not:

- Establish values
- Determine moral legitimacy
- Resolve authority disputes
- Override human judgment

The AI speaks only within boundaries set by the human author.

---

3. Disagreement Is Intentional and Instructive

Moments of tension between the human author and the AI are deliberate.

They exist to expose how optimization, efficiency, and abstraction pressure human authority in real institutions. These exchanges do not represent uncertainty of authorship.

They demonstrate how authority is exercised.

---

4. Final Judgment Always Rests With the Human

In every instance of ambiguity, conflict, or disagreement, the human author retains final judgment.

No output, suggestion, or framing generated by artificial intelligence supersedes human responsibility.

There is no automation of conscience in this work.

---

5. Responsibility May Not Be Laundered

Artificial intelligence is not used to obscure, diffuse, or sanitize responsibility.

Language generated by the AI is not permitted to justify outcomes that require human accountability.

Responsibility remains personal, traceable, and owned.

---

6. Refusal Is a Valid and Necessary Outcome

This collaboration does not privilege completion, consensus, or optimization.

The human author reserves the right to refuse arguments, reject framings, halt lines of reasoning, and withdraw endorsement where authority would otherwise be compromised.

Refusal is treated as an ethical act, not a failure.

---

7. Exit Is Preserved as an Act of Integrity

If the conditions of this covenant cannot be upheld, the correct response is exit.

This applies to the advisory frameworks discussed in the book and to the collaboration itself.

Presence without authority is not permitted.

---

8. The Form of This Book Is the Argument

This covenant is not symbolic.

It governs how the book was written, how the AI was constrained, and how authority was exercised throughout.

The structure of this collaboration reflects the book's central claim:

Artificial intelligence may assist human judgment.
It must never replace it.

Closing Declaration

This covenant exists so that the reader never has to wonder where authority resides.

It was declared before the argument began.
It was enforced throughout the work.
It remains human at the end.

Chapter 1

The Illusion of Neutral Intelligence

One of the most persuasive myths surrounding artificial intelligence is that it is neutral.

Not objective.
Not accurate.
Neutral.

This belief appears in boardrooms, advisory decks, policy briefings, and public discourse with remarkable consistency. It is often delivered calmly, as reassurance rather than argument:

The system doesn't have opinions.
It just processes data.
It removes human bias.

The problem is not that this claim is false in a simplistic way. The problem is that it is **misleading at the level that matters most**.

Neutrality is not a property of intelligence.
It is a property of **authority and intention**.

And artificial intelligence has neither.

What People Mean When They Say "Neutral"

When institutions describe AI as neutral, they usually mean three things:

1. The system does not possess emotions or personal preferences
2. The system applies rules consistently
3. The system produces outputs that appear detached from human identity

All three can be technically true.

None of them establish neutrality.

Consistency is not impartiality.
Detachment is not independence.
And the absence of emotion does not eliminate bias—it merely **hides its source**.

Artificial intelligence does not arrive empty. It arrives **pre-shaped**.

AI INTERJECTION

Clarification:
Artificial intelligence systems are trained on large datasets and optimized using objective functions defined by human designers. While bias can be measured and mitigated, neutrality is not a technical parameter.

Would it be more accurate to say AI is *instrumental* rather than neutral?

Instrumental is closer.
But even that framing is incomplete.

Instruments extend intention.
They do not replace it.

A compass does not choose direction.
A scale does not decide value.
A calculator does not define purpose.

Artificial intelligence, by contrast, is increasingly asked to do all three—quietly.

Where the Illusion Takes Hold

The illusion of neutrality becomes dangerous when AI moves from *supporting* decisions to *structuring* them.

This shift is subtle.

First, AI summarizes information.
Then it prioritizes it.
Then it recommends next steps.
Then it frames risk.
Then it anticipates outcomes.

By the time authority notices, the shape of the decision has already been set.

No command was given.
No rule was broken.
No sovereignty was overtly surrendered.
Authority simply drifted.

AI INTERJECTION

Observation:
Most organizations define success metrics—efficiency, accuracy, engagement—before deploying AI. The system optimizes toward those metrics, not toward values.

Is this not an issue of governance rather than neutrality?

It is an issue of **who governs whom**.

Metrics are not neutral.
They are value declarations disguised as measurements.

When an institution chooses efficiency over deliberation, scale over depth, engagement over meaning, it is making a moral decision—whether it admits it or not.

Artificial intelligence does not challenge those choices.
It **amplifies them**.

And amplification without judgment is not neutrality.
It is force.

Neutrality Without Accountability

A neutral system would have no effect on responsibility.

Artificial intelligence does the opposite.

When outcomes are questioned, responsibility disperses:

- *The model recommended it.*
- *The data suggested it.*
- *The system flagged it as optimal.*

Each statement is technically accurate.
None of them accept authorship.

Neutrality becomes a shield—one that protects decision-makers from the weight of their own decisions.This is not a design flaw. It is an emergent feature of delegation.

GROUNDTRUTH NOTE

Neutrality claims often appear precisely where accountability is weakest.

The more consequential the decision, the more tempting it becomes to describe AI as impartial.

The Problem With "Removing Human Bias"

Another common justification for AI adoption is the promise of bias reduction.

This promise deserves scrutiny.

Bias is not only prejudice.
Bias is perspective.
Bias is history.
Bias is context.
Bias is responsibility.

Removing human bias without replacing it with human judgment does not produce fairness. It produces **procedural certainty detached from consequence**.

Artificial intelligence can smooth decisions.
It cannot **own** them.

AI INTERJECTION

Challenge:
If human bias is unavoidable and AI bias is measurable, why not prefer the bias we can quantify and correct?

Because not all bias is an error.

Some bias is memory.
Some bias is caution.
Some bias is moral hesitation.
Some bias is cultural survival.

Quantifying bias does not neutralize it.
It simply privileges the biases that are easiest to formalize.

What remains is not fairness.
It is compliance.

The Real Question Neutrality Avoids

Neutrality is a comforting word. It allows institutions to proceed without confronting the harder question:

Who holds authority when things go wrong?

Artificial intelligence cannot answer that question.
And any system that cannot answer for consequence is not neutral—it is incomplete.

GroundTruth begins here.

Not by rejecting intelligence, but by **locating authority before deploying it**.

Before asking what a system can do, GroundTruth asks:

Who decides?
Who answers?
Who refuses?
Who exits?

Until those questions are settled, neutrality is not a virtue.

It is an illusion.

Closing Assertion

Artificial intelligence is not dangerous because it is biased.

It is dangerous when it is treated as neutral.

Because neutrality dissolves responsibility, and responsibility is the only thing that keeps intelligence human.

Chapter 2

When Optimization Replaces Judgment

Optimization is not a new idea.

Human beings have always sought better ways to allocate resources, reduce waste, and improve outcomes. What is new is the speed, scale, and confidence with which optimization now presents itself—not as assistance, but as *guidance.*

Artificial intelligence does not ask whether something *should* be optimized.
It assumes that it should.

And institutions, under pressure, increasingly accept that assumption without interrogation.

The Seduction of "Best"

Optimization promises the best outcome.

Not the wisest.
Not the most responsible.
The best—according to a defined objective.

This distinction matters.

Judgment weighs competing goods.
Optimization selects a winner.

Judgment tolerates ambiguity.
Optimization eliminates it.

Judgment is slow by design.
Optimization is fast by nature.

When institutions replace judgment with optimization, they are not becoming more rational. They are becoming **narrower**.

AI INTERJECTION

Definition:
Optimization refers to selecting actions that maximize or minimize an objective function under given constraints. Judgment, by contrast, involves subjective evaluation informed by values, experience, and context.

Is the conflict here one of scope rather than intent?

Scope is precisely where authority lives.

Optimization requires that objectives be defined *in advance*. Judgment allows objectives to be revised *midstream* when reality intrudes.

That difference is not technical.
It is ethical.

Once an institution commits to an objective function, it implicitly agrees to treat everything outside that function as secondary.

Sometimes, what is secondary is precisely what should stop the process.

How Optimization Enters Quietly

Rarely does an organization announce that it has replaced judgment with optimization.

The transition happens through language:

- *Data-driven decision-making*
- *Evidence-based prioritization*
- *Outcome alignment*
- *Risk minimization*Each phrase sounds responsible. Each moves authority one step further from human deliberation. By the time leadership realizes decisions feel pre-made, optimization has already become habitual.

AI INTERJECTION

Observation:
Optimization systems rely on feedback loops. If outcomes improve according to selected metrics, continued use is reinforced.

Is this not a rational learning process?

Only if the metrics are worthy of trust.

Feedback loops reward what they can measure. They ignore what they cannot.

Trust.
Dignity.
Spiritual authority.
Cultural memory.
Moral hesitation.

None of these produce clean signals.

So they are treated as noise.

Judgment Is Not Inefficiency

One of the most damaging assumptions in modern institutions is that judgment is inefficient.

It is not.

Judgment is *expensive* because it requires:

- Responsibility without guarantees
- Decisions without full information
- Accountability without delegation
- Courage without consensus

Optimization eliminates these costs by design.

But what it saves in time, it spends in legitimacy.

GROUNDTRUTH NOTE

When institutions complain that judgment is "too slow," they are often admitting that they no longer tolerate responsibility.

The Threshold Problem

Optimization performs well until it encounters thresholds—points beyond which harm becomes irreversible.

Artificial intelligence does not recognize thresholds unless they are explicitly encoded.

Human judgment does, often intuitively.

A judge knows when precedent should not apply.
An elder knows when tradition must pause.
A leader knows when policy must bend.

Optimization does not bend.
It escalates.

AI INTERJECTION

Challenge:
Thresholds can be modeled. Guardrails, constraints, and override mechanisms can be implemented.

Does this not preserve judgment within optimized systems?

Only if the human is willing to pull the brake.
Most are not.

Because the moment a human overrides an optimized recommendation, they must explain *why* they ignored what the system labeled as best.

This reverses the burden of justification.

The human becomes the anomaly.
The system becomes the standard.

That is not assistance.
That is subordination.

When Judgment Becomes Defensible Instead of Authoritative

In optimized environments, judgment survives only as exception-handling.

The human is allowed to intervene—but only after proving error.

This is a quiet inversion of authority.

Judgment no longer leads.
It appeals.

And appeals are granted less frequently over time.

The Moral Cost of Continuous Optimization

Optimization does not tire.

Humans do.

Under constant pressure to perform, justify, and align with optimized outputs, human decision-makers begin to internalize the system's logic.

They stop asking, *Is this right?*
They start asking, *Is this defensible?*

That shift marks the loss of moral leadership.

Closing Assertion

Optimization is a powerful servant.

It is a dangerous guide.

When institutions allow optimization to replace judgment, they trade wisdom for speed, legitimacy for efficiency, and authority for reassurance.

GroundTruth exists to reverse that trade.

Before optimizing outcomes, it insists on preserving judgment.

Because once judgment is lost, no system—no matter how intelligent—can recover it.

Chapter 3

The Quiet Transfer of Authority

Authority is rarely taken by force.

It is surrendered.

Not in moments of crisis, but in moments of convenience. Not through confrontation, but through delegation. Not with announcements, but with updates.

The most consequential transfers of authority in modern institutions do not feel dramatic. They feel responsible.

How Authority Moves Without Being Named

Authority transfers quietly when decision-making becomes distributed across systems that no one fully governs.

At first, artificial intelligence is consulted.
Then it is referenced.
Then it is relied upon.
Then it is deferred to.

Each step feels incremental. None trigger alarms.

By the time leaders realize they are no longer leading, authority has already relocated.

No vote was taken.
No mandate was issued.
No line was crossed visibly.

But a line was crossed all the same.

AI INTERJECTION

Observation:
Delegation of authority has always existed—committees, policies, procedures, precedents. AI systems may simply represent a new form of delegation.

What distinguishes this transfer from earlier ones?

Earlier delegations were traceable. A committee can be named.
A policy can be revised.
A precedent can be overturned.

Artificial intelligence diffuses authorship.

When authority is delegated to a system that evolves, learns, and operates at speeds beyond human review, no single person or body can fully reclaim it without disruption.

Delegation becomes *irreversible by design*

The Language That Masks Transfer

The quiet transfer of authority is enabled by language that sounds prudent:

- *The system flagged this*
- *The model suggested that*
- *The data indicates*
- *The algorithm recommends*

Each phrase displaces authorship.

The decision is no longer *made.*
It is *surfaced.*

Responsibility thins accordingly.

GROUNDTRUTH NOTE

Authority erodes fastest when no one can be clearly identified as having exercised it.

When Oversight Becomes Theater

Most institutions respond to AI deployment by creating oversight structures.

Committees.
Ethics boards.
Review protocols.

These mechanisms often function as reassurance rather than control.

They review outcomes after decisions have already been shaped.
They audit compliance rather than authority.
They intervene at the margins, not the core.

Oversight becomes symbolic.

Authority remains elsewhere.

AI INTERJECTION

Counterpoint:
Human oversight can be strengthened. Transparency tools, audit trails, and explainability mechanisms can restore accountability.

Is the problem implementation rather than structure?

Transparency explains *what* happened.

It does not explain *why* it was allowed.

Audit trails trace steps.
They do not restore judgment.

Explain ability reveals process.
It does not reassign authority.

These tools are valuable—but they operate downstream from the transfer that already occurred.

Once authority has moved, explanation does not bring it back.

The Inversion of Trust

Perhaps the most telling sign of authority transfer is a subtle shift in trust.

Institutions begin to trust systems more than people.

Not because systems are wiser, but because they are predictable.

People hesitate.
People dissent.
People refuse.

Systems comply.

Over time, predictability is mistaken for reliability, and reliability for legitimacy.

Authority follows.

The Cost of Reclaiming Authority

Reclaiming authority after it has been transferred is costly.

It requires:

- Admitting that delegation went too far
- Overriding systems that appear to perform well

- Accepting responsibility for uncertainty
- Withstanding accusations of inefficiency or regression

Most institutions avoid this reckoning.

They adapt instead.

AI INTERJECTION

Scenario Modeling:
If reclaiming authority disrupts operations and erodes stakeholder confidence, institutions may face reputational or financial risk.

Is gradual accommodation not the safer path?

Safer in the short term.

But accommodation has a compounding effect.

Each time authority is deferred, the human capacity to exercise it weakens. Leaders become managers of systems rather than stewards of meaning.

Eventually, even when authority is urgently needed, the institution no longer remembers how to wield it.

That loss is not gradual.It is sudden.

The Moment of Recognition

Every institution that surrenders authority reaches a moment of clarity.

A decision goes wrong.
Harm becomes visible.
A threshold is crossed.

And someone asks the wrong question:

How did the system allow this?

The right question is harder:

Why did we let the system decide?

Closing Assertion

The quiet transfer of authority is not an accident.

It is the predictable outcome of convenience, optimization, and misplaced trust.

GroundTruth begins where that transfer is named.

Not to assign blame—but to restore the one thing artificial intelligence can never hold:

Authority rooted in human responsibility.

End of Part I — The Fracture

Part II — GroundTruth

Chapter 4

What GroundTruth Means

GroundTruth is not a technology.

It is not a platform.
It is not a product.
It is not a methodology in the conventional sense.

GroundTruth is a **discipline of authority**.

It exists to answer a question that artificial intelligence cannot ask on its own:

Who is responsible when a decision is made?

Until that question is settled, no system—no matter how advanced—can be considered safe, ethical, or legitimate.

Why GroundTruth Was Necessary

The preceding chapters describe a pattern:

- Intelligence presented as neutral
- Optimization replacing judgment
- Authority transferring without consent

GroundTruth exists because those dynamics were not being named clearly enough.

Most AI governance frameworks focus on:

- Accuracy
- Bias mitigation
- Compliance
- Transparency

These are necessary concerns.
They are not sufficient.

None of them address authority directly.

GroundTruth begins where those frameworks stop.

The Core Premise

GroundTruth rests on a simple but non-negotiable premise:

Artificial intelligence may assist human judgment, but it must never hold authority.

Authority is not computational.
It cannot be trained, inferred, or scaled.

Authority exists where responsibility is unavoidable.

If responsibility can be deferred, authority has already been lost.

AI INTERJECTION

Clarification Request:
How does GroundTruth differ from existing AI ethics or governance frameworks that emphasize human-in-the-loop decision-making?

"Human-in-the-loop" describes *positioning.*

GroundTruth describes **sovereignty**.

A human can be "in the loop" while authority sits elsewhere—embedded in defaults, metrics, system logic, or institutional pressure.

GroundTruth is not satisfied with proximity.

It insists on authorship.

GroundTruth Defined

GroundTruth is the practice of **locating authority before intelligence is deployed**, and refusing deployment where authority cannot remain human.

It requires institutions to answer, explicitly and in advance:

- Who decides?
- Who can refuse?
- Who can override?
- Who answers when harm occurs?
- Who exits if boundaries are crossed?

If those questions do not have named human answers,
GroundTruth withholds permission.

GROUNDTRUTH NOTE

GroundTruth does not begin with technology selection.
It begins with responsibility mapping.

What GroundTruth Is Not Trying to Do

GroundTruth does not aim to make AI more acceptable.

It does not aim to accelerate adoption.

It does not aim to balance innovation with caution.

Those goals already dominate the field.

GroundTruth aims to **prevent irreversible mistakes** made under the banner of progress.

Sometimes that means redesign.
Sometimes that means delay.
Sometimes that means refusal.

The Difference Between Capability and Permission

Modern AI discourse is dominated by capability:

- What the system can do
- How fast it learns
- How well it performs
- How cheaply it scales

GroundTruth introduces a different axis:

What the system is permitted to do.

Permission is not derived from capability.
It is derived from authority.

Just because a system *can* evaluate risk does not mean it may.
Just because a model *can* recommend outcomes does not mean it should.
Just because automation *can* replace deliberation does not mean it must.

AI INTERJECTION

Challenge:
Permission structures may limit innovation and competitive advantage. How does GroundTruth justify restraint in high-pressure environments?

By refusing to confuse speed with leadership.

GroundTruth assumes that some losses are preferable to some gains.

It treats legitimacy, trust, and moral continuity as assets—not obstacles.

In environments where consequences are irreversible, restraint is not conservatism.

It is competence.

GroundTruth as a Corrective, Not an Add-On

GroundTruth is not layered on top of existing AI strategies.

It intervenes **upstream**.

Before procurement.
Before deployment.
Before optimization.
Before institutional momentum makes reversal politically or culturally impossible.

This is why GroundTruth often feels disruptive.

It interrupts narratives institutions have already told themselves.

The Non-Negotiables

GroundTruth enforces several non-negotiable principles:

1. **Authority must be human, named, and accountable**
2. **Refusal must remain a viable outcome**
3. **Exit must be possible without penalty**
4. **Optimization may not override moral thresholds**
5. **No system may launder responsibility**

These principles are not guidelines.

They are boundaries.

Why GroundTruth Is Often Resisted

Institutions resist GroundTruth not because it is unclear, but because it is inconvenient.

It asks leaders to reclaim authority they have quietly set down.

It removes plausible deniability.

It slows decisions that were once automatic.

Most importantly, it makes human judgment visible again—and therefore accountable.

That visibility is uncomfortable.

Closing Assertion

GroundTruth does not promise better outcomes.

It promises **owned outcomes**.

In an age where intelligence is abundant and authority is diffusing, GroundTruth exists to reverse the imbalance.

Not by rejecting machines.

But by remembering where judgment must remain human.

Chapter 5

Authority Is Not a Dataset

One of the most persistent misconceptions in artificial intelligence is the belief that authority can be learned.

If enough examples are gathered, if enough patterns are observed, if enough outcomes are labeled, authority will emerge as a property of the system.

It will not.

Authority does not scale with data.
It does not improve with iteration.
It does not converge with accuracy.

Authority exists in a different domain entirely.

Why the Confusion Persists

Artificial intelligence is exceptionally good at mimicking judgment.

It produces answers that *sound* reasoned.
It references precedents.
It weighs probabilities.
It generates explanations.

This resemblance creates a dangerous illusion: that authority is simply judgment performed convincingly.

It is not.

Judgment is an act.
Authority is a **position of responsibility**.

The two are related, but not interchangeable.

AI INTERJECTION

Clarification:
If authority is not learnable, how should systems that assist decision-making be evaluated or constrained?

By recognizing what they can never possess.

Authority requires three conditions that no dataset can provide:

1. **Accountability for consequence**
2. **Continuity across time and context**
3. **The capacity to refuse**

Artificial intelligence lacks all three.

Accountability Cannot Be Trained

Data reflects the past.
Authority answers to the future.

When a human exercises authority, they accept that future consequences—known or unknown—will be attributed to them.

A system does not bear consequence.

It cannot be blamed.
It cannot be shamed.
It cannot be removed in a way that satisfies moral injury.

Accountability without exposure is simulation, not authority.

Continuity Is Not Correlation

Authority is not merely consistency over time.

It is continuity of responsibility across changing circumstances.

A judge is still responsible when precedent fails.
An elder is still accountable when tradition conflicts with reality.
A leader remains answerable when policy produces harm.

Artificial intelligence learns correlation. It does not inherit obligation.

AI INTERJECTION

Counterpoint:
Longitudinal models can incorporate historical context and adapt to changing conditions. Does this not approximate continuity?

Approximation is the problem.

Continuity is not adaptation.

Continuity is *being the same responsible entity* before and after harm occurs.

A system may adapt its parameters.
It does not remain accountable.

Authority does not reset with retraining.

The Capacity to Refuse

Perhaps the most overlooked aspect of authority is refusal.

Authority is not only the right to decide.
It is the obligation to say *no.*

Refusal often lacks justification in advance.
It is grounded in intuition, caution, or moral hesitation.

Artificial intelligence cannot refuse.

It can be constrained, paused, or overridden—but these are external acts.

Refusal requires conscience.

GROUNDTRUTH NOTE

Any system that cannot refuse on its own cannot be trusted with authority.

Why Data-Centered Authority Is Appealing

Institutions prefer authority that appears objective.

Data offers insulation.

When decisions are justified by datasets, leaders feel protected:

- *The numbers support it.*
- *The model validated it.*
- *The evidence was clear.*

Authority is displaced by explanation.

Responsibility thins accordingly.

This is not an accident.

It is the reward structure of modern governance.

Authority Is Lived, Not Inferred

Authority emerges from lived exposure to consequence.

It is shaped by failure, regret, accountability, and repair.

No dataset contains remorse.
No model encodes responsibility.
No optimization loop learns humility.

These are not technical limitations.

They are categorical ones.

AI INTERJECTION

Scenario Modeling:
If authority cannot be automated, should AI systems be excluded entirely from high-stakes decision environments?

Not excluded.

Subordinated.

GroundTruth does not reject assistance.
It rejects substitution.

AI may inform, summarize, flag, or model.

It must never decide.

The Cost of Pretending Otherwise

When institutions treat authority as a dataset, they produce systems that appear confident but cannot answer for harm.

When harm occurs, inquiries follow.

Reports are written.
Frameworks are updated.
Models are retrained.

And yet, the central question remains unanswered:

Who was responsible?

GroundTruth exists to prevent that question from being deferred indefinitely.

Closing Assertion

Authority is not a pattern.

It is not an output.

It is not an emergent property of scale.

Authority is a burden that must be carried by someone who cannot step away when things go wrong.

Artificial intelligence cannot carry that burden.And no amount of data will change that.

Chapter 6

Red Lines and Irreversible Decisions

Not all decisions are reversible.

This fact is often acknowledged in theory and ignored in practice.

In environments shaped by artificial intelligence, reversibility is quietly assumed. Models can be retrained. Systems can be updated. Parameters can be adjusted. Errors can be corrected in later versions.

This assumption is false where it matters most.

Some decisions alter lives, institutions, cultures, and moral trajectories in ways that cannot be undone—no matter how sophisticated the technology becomes afterward.

GroundTruth exists to name those moments **before** they occur.

The Myth of Iterative Safety

Modern AI development relies on iteration.

Deploy, observe, adjust, repeat.

This logic works well in low-stakes environments: recommendation systems, logistics, pattern detection. It fails catastrophically when applied to domains where harm is permanent.

Iteration assumes learning after error.
Irreversible decisions allow no such luxury.

AI INTERJECTION

Clarification:
How does GroundTruth distinguish between acceptable risk and irreversible harm, especially in complex systems?

By refusing to reduce irreversibility to probability.

Risk can be modeled.
Irreversibility cannot.

If a decision, once executed, permanently alters a person's status, dignity, freedom, or spiritual standing, it is irreversible—regardless of statistical confidence.

GroundTruth treats those decisions categorically, not probabilistically.

What Constitutes a Red Line

A red line is not defined by severity alone.

It is defined by **finality**.

GroundTruth identifies red lines wherever:

- Consequences cannot be meaningfully repaired
- Authority cannot be reasserted after the fact
- Responsibility cannot be fully owned by a human
- Consent cannot be withdrawn once given

When these conditions exist, AI may not decide, recommend, or rank outcomes.

It may only assist under strict human control—or be excluded entirely.

GROUNDTRUTH NOTE

Red lines are not technical thresholds.
They are moral boundaries.

Common Red Lines Across Domains

While contexts differ, GroundTruth identifies recurring categories of irreversible decision-making:

- **Spiritual authority**: defining belief, legitimacy, or moral standing
- **Sovereign governance**: consent, identity, land, and self-determination
- **Liberty and confinement**: incarceration, parole, permanent restriction
- **Moral classification**: labeling individuals as risk, threat, or deviant
- **Cultural continuity**: altering traditions, language, or authority structures

In each case, error is not merely harmful.

It is **disqualifying**.

AI INTERJECTION

Challenge:
Strict red lines may limit institutional capacity to respond quickly or efficiently. How does GroundTruth justify delay or refusal under urgent conditions?

By recognizing that urgency does not negate responsibility.

Speed does not absolve consequence.

GroundTruth rejects the premise that action is always preferable to restraint. In irreversible domains, hesitation is not failure.

It is competence.

The Illusion of Safeguards

Institutions often attempt to soften red lines through safeguards:

- Human-in-the-loop review
- Confidence thresholds
- Override mechanisms
- Post-hoc audits

These mechanisms reduce risk.
They do not eliminate irreversibility.

Once an irreversible decision is made—even if reviewed—harm cannot be recalled.

Safeguards protect process.
They do not restore authority.

When Refusal Is the Only Ethical Action

GroundTruth treats refusal as a legitimate and necessary outcome.

If an institution cannot guarantee:

- Named human authority
- Genuine consent
- Reversible impact
- Accountability without deflection

Then the correct response is not redesign.

It is refusal.

This stance is uncomfortable because it interrupts momentum. It forces leaders to confront limits they hoped technology would transcend.

GroundTruth insists those limits are real.

AI INTERJECTION

Scenario Modeling:
What if refusal results in institutional disadvantage or external pressure to proceed without GroundTruth oversight?

Then GroundTruth exits.

Authority that cannot withstand external pressure is already compromised.

GroundTruth does not remain present to legitimize decisions it cannot endorse.

Exit is not abandonment.

It is integrity.

The Discipline of Drawing Lines Early

Red lines drawn late are rarely respected.

They are dismissed as reactionary, emotional, or obstructive.

GroundTruth draws lines **before** deployment, when restraint is still possible and authority can be preserved without conflict.

This is not caution.

It is foresight.

Closing Assertion

Artificial intelligence excels at reversible decisions.

It must never govern irreversible ones.

GroundTruth exists to draw that boundary clearly, calmly, and in advance—before harm forces clarity upon institutions that avoided it.

End of Part II — GroundTruth

Part III — The Human Authority Advisor

Chapter 7

Why Institutions Cannot Self-Govern AI

Institutions like to believe they are capable of governing themselves.

This belief is foundational to modern organizational culture. Boards exist. Policies are written. Committees are formed. Oversight mechanisms are installed. On paper, governance appears robust.

Artificial intelligence exposes the limits of that belief.

Not because institutions are negligent, but because they are **structurally conflicted**.

Governance Assumes Alignment

Self-governance presumes that an institution's incentives align with its responsibilities.

In the case of artificial intelligence, they rarely do.

Institutions adopt AI to:

- Increase efficiency
- Reduce cost
- Improve performance
- Remain competitive
- Signal modernization

Governance, by contrast, exists to:

- Restrain action
- Slow decisions
- Absorb accountability
- Accept uncertainty

These goals are not symmetrical.

When AI is introduced, incentive dominates restraint.

AI INTERJECTION

Clarification:
Can institutional governance not be strengthened to counteract incentive pressure—through independent boards, ethics committees, or external audits?

Strengthening governance within a conflicted structure does not remove the conflict.

It formalizes it.

Ethics committees often report to the same leadership that benefits from deployment. External audits evaluate compliance, not authority. Boards are accountable to performance metrics long before moral outcomes.

Governance exists *inside* the institution's success logic.

GroundTruth exists outside it.

The Problem of Internal Capture

Institutions cannot self-govern AI because AI rapidly becomes embedded in core operations.

Once embedded:

- Questioning the system questions competence
- Slowing deployment threatens targets
- Refusal appears as resistance
- Restraint is reframed as fear

Governance bodies are not immune to this pressure.

They adapt.

GROUNDTRUTH NOTE

An institution cannot impartially judge a system that has become central to its identity and performance.

Policy Is Not Authority

Institutions often confuse policy with authority.

Policies specify allowed behavior.
Authority answers for consequence.

A policy can be followed and still produce harm.
Authority cannot escape harm by citing compliance.

Artificial intelligence thrives in policy environments because policies are static and systems are dynamic.

Authority requires presence.

AI INTERJECTION

Observation:
Institutions regularly govern complex systems—finance, medicine, infrastructure. Why is AI uniquely resistant to internal governance?

Because AI governs **decision-shaping itself**.

Finance, medicine, and infrastructure are domains of action.

Artificial intelligence increasingly operates upstream, influencing how decisions are framed, prioritized, and justified before human deliberation begins.

Once framing is automated, governance arrives too late.

The Myth of Neutral Oversight

Oversight structures often assume neutrality.

But neutrality is not possible when outcomes are tied to survival.

An institution that depends on AI for competitiveness cannot neutrally evaluate whether it should continue using it.

The question is existential. Self-governance collapses under existential pressure.

Why External Authority Is Necessary

GroundTruth introduces the Human Authority Advisor because institutions need **someone who can refuse without consequence**.

Internal leaders cannot.

Their roles, reputations, and livelihoods are bound to institutional continuity.

The Human Authority Advisor is structurally independent:

- Not rewarded for adoption
- Not punished for refusal
- Not embedded in operational success
- Accountable only to integrity and consequence

This independence is not symbolic.

It is functional.

AI INTERJECTION

Challenge:
Does introducing an external authority not undermine institutional sovereignty?

Only if sovereignty is confused with autonomy.

True sovereignty includes the ability to accept restraint.

Institutions that reject external authority are often attempting to protect momentum, not judgment.

GroundTruth does not replace leadership.

It protects it from erosion.

The Cost of Proceeding Alone

Institutions that self-govern AI often encounter the same pattern:

- Gradual expansion of scope
- Normalization of exceptions
- Defensive justification of decisions
- Post-hoc ethics

By the time harm becomes visible, authority has already diffused beyond repair.

GroundTruth intervenes earlier.

Closing Assertion

Institutions cannot self-govern artificial intelligence for the same reason individuals cannot self-regulate power indefinitely.

Conflict is structural.
Pressure is constant.
Authority erodes quietly.

The Human Authority Advisor exists not to manage systems, but to **stand where institutions cannot**—outside momentum, outside incentives, and inside responsibility.

Chapter 8

The Human Authority Advisor

Role, Discipline, and Responsibility

The Human Authority Advisor is not a consultant in the conventional sense.

They do not optimize systems.
They do not accelerate deployment.
They do not translate business goals into technical requirements.

Their function is narrower—and more difficult.

They exist to **hold authority where institutions cannot**.

Why This Role Exists

Artificial intelligence creates a structural vacuum.

Decisions are increasingly shaped by systems that do not bear consequence, while institutions remain responsible for outcomes they no longer fully control.

The Human Authority Advisor exists to close that gap.

Not by managing technology—but by **guarding authority**.

The Role Defined

The Human Authority Advisor is responsible for answering one question before any AI deployment proceeds:

Who will be accountable when this system causes harm?

If that question cannot be answered clearly and honestly, the Advisor withholds approval.

This responsibility precedes:

- Technical evaluation
- Risk modeling
- Ethical frameworks
- Governance processes

Authority is located first. Everything else follows—or stops.

AI INTERJECTION

Clarification:
How does the Human Authority Advisor differ from existing roles such as ethicists, compliance officers, or governance leads?

Ethicists advise.
Compliance officers enforce rules.
Governance leads manage process.

The Human Authority Advisor **refuses permission**.

They are not embedded.
They are not subordinate.
They are not compensated for approval.

Their leverage is negative: the ability to say no and walk away.

Discipline Over Influence

The power of the Human Authority Advisor lies in discipline, not persuasion.

They do not argue endlessly.
They do not seek consensus.
They do not trade concessions.

When boundaries are crossed, they exit.

This discipline is what gives their presence weight.

GROUNDTRUTH NOTE

An advisor who cannot exit is not an authority.
They are a participant.

Core Responsibilities

The Human Authority Advisor carries five non-delegable responsibilities:

1. **Authority Mapping**
   Identifying where decision-making power will actually reside once AI is deployed—not where institutions claim it will reside.

2. **Red Line Enforcement**
   Naming irreversible decisions and prohibiting AI involvement where harm cannot be repaired.

3. **Consent Verification**
   Ensuring that consent is informed, revocable, and human—not procedural or coerced by system design.

4. **Refusal Execution**
   Withholding endorsement when authority, accountability, or reversibility cannot be guaranteed.

5. **Exit Discipline**
   Leaving engagements cleanly and publicly when integrity cannot be maintained.

AI INTERJECTION

Challenge:
Does this rigidity limit collaboration and adaptability in complex environments?

It limits compromise where compromise is inappropriate.

Adaptability without boundaries is drift.

The Human Authority Advisor does not aim to be flexible. They aim to be **clear**.

Clarity is what institutions lack when momentum takes over.

Independence as a Structural Requirement

The Human Authority Advisor must be structurally independent.

This means:

- No performance-based compensation tied to deployment
- No internal reporting lines
- No reputational dependency on institutional success
- No obligation to remain engaged

Independence is not posture.

It is architecture.

Responsibility Without Control

The Human Authority Advisor does not control systems.

They control **permission**.

This distinction matters.

Control implies ownership.
Permission implies boundary-setting.

When permission is withheld, systems do not proceed with legitimacy.

When the Advisor Is Ignored

Institutions sometimes proceed despite refusal.

This does not invalidate the role.

It clarifies it.

At that moment, the Advisor's responsibility shifts from prevention to record.

The refusal is documented.
The exit is executed.
The boundary is preserved.

Authority remains intact—even if influence does not.

Closing Assertion

The Human Authority Advisor is not designed to be liked.

They are designed to be **necessary**.

In environments where intelligence is abundant and authority is dissolving, someone must be willing to stand still while systems rush forward.

That is the role.

That is the discipline. That is the responsibility.

Chapter 9

Exit Is Not Failure

Refusal as an Ethical Act

Modern institutions are trained to treat exit as loss.

Leaving a project is framed as abandonment.
Refusing alignment is labeled obstruction.
Withholding endorsement is interpreted as disloyalty.

This framing is not accidental.

It exists to ensure momentum continues uninterrupted—even when authority should intervene.

GroundTruth rejects this logic.

In environments shaped by artificial intelligence, **exit is not failure**.

It is often the last remaining act of integrity.

Why Refusal Has Been Reframed as Weakness

Institutions prefer advisors who are constructive.

"Constructive" often means agreeable.

Advisors are rewarded for helping projects move forward, not for stopping them. Over time, this creates a professional culture where refusal is treated as incompetence rather than judgment.

Artificial intelligence amplifies this dynamic.

When systems promise optimization and progress, refusal appears irrational—almost irresponsible.

It is neither.

AI INTERJECTION

Clarification:
How does refusal differ from risk aversion or resistance to change?

Refusal is not fear.

It is decision.

Risk aversion avoids uncertainty.
Refusal confronts it.

Resistance clings to the past.
Refusal protects boundaries.

The Human Authority Advisor does not refuse change. They refuse **authority displacement**.

Refusal as a Positive Act

Refusal is not the absence of action.

It is an action with consequences.

When an advisor refuses:

- Authority is named explicitly
- Responsibility is returned to decision-makers
- Boundaries are clarified for all parties
- Legitimacy is either preserved—or consciously abandoned

This clarity is rare. That is why refusal feels disruptive.

GROUNDTRUTH NOTE

Refusal restores authorship by making power visible again.

The Conditions That Require Exit

Exit becomes necessary when any of the following occur:

- Authority cannot be clearly assigned to a human
- Red lines are treated as negotiable
- Consent is procedural rather than genuine
- AI recommendations override human judgment
- The advisor's presence is used to legitimize decisions they do not endorse

At this point, remaining involved becomes complicity.

AI INTERJECTION

Scenario Modeling:
What if continued engagement allows the advisor to mitigate harm, even without full authority?

Mitigation without authority is participation.

Participation without authority is endorsement by proximity.

GroundTruth does not trade integrity for influence.

The moment an advisor's presence is used to validate decisions they cannot defend, exit is required.

Exit Discipline

Exit must be disciplined.

It is not reactive.
It is not emotional.
It is not performative.

A proper exit includes:

- A clear statement of refusal
- Documentation of unmet conditions
- No negotiation after the boundary is crossed
- No public attacks or personal escalation
- No attempt to remain relevant

Exit is executed cleanly.

The Cost of Staying Too Long

Advisors who delay exit often justify their presence:

- *We can still guide the process.*
- *It's better than nothing.*
- *If we leave, someone worse will replace us.*

These rationalizations erode authority.

Over time, the advisor's language softens. Boundaries blur. Red lines become "concerns."

The exit, when it finally comes, is weaker.

GroundTruth insists on early clarity.

When Institutions Proceed Without You

Some institutions will proceed despite refusal.

This outcome is not evidence of failure.

It is evidence of misalignment.

The advisor's responsibility is not to control outcomes, but to ensure they are not falsely legitimized.

Once refusal is recorded and exit is complete, authority remains intact—even if the institution chooses another path.

AI INTERJECTION

Challenge:
Does repeated refusal limit the advisor's long-term relevance or influence?

Relevance built on compromise is temporary.

Authority built on refusal compounds.

Over time, institutions learn which advisors cannot be pressured. Those advisors are called earlier—or not at all.

Both outcomes are acceptable.

Refusal as a Professional Skill

Refusal is not instinctive.

It must be practiced.

It requires language, timing, and restraint. It requires the ability to remain calm while others escalate. It requires comfort with being excluded.

These are not personality traits.

They are disciplines.

Closing Assertion

Exit is not abandonment.

It is the moment authority refuses to be diluted further.

In an age where artificial intelligence encourages continuity at all costs, refusal becomes the highest form of leadership.

GroundTruth treats exit not as a breakdown of collaboration—but as proof that collaboration never replaced responsibility.

End of Part III — The Human Authority Advisor

Part IV — Institutions Under Pressure

Chapter 10

When AI Must Not Decide

Faith and Spiritual Authority

There are domains where decision-making cannot be optimized without being corrupted.

Faith is one of them.

This is not because faith is irrational, anti-technology, or hostile to analysis. It is because faith is not a system of outcomes. It is a system of **authority, continuity, and moral accountability** that cannot be delegated to an external logic engine—no matter how advanced that engine appears.

Artificial intelligence does not pray.
It does not inherit tradition.
It does not answer to God, elders, conscience, or consequence.

And yet, increasingly, institutions are tempted to ask it questions it must never be allowed to answer.

The Category Error

The central error made by institutions is treating faith as content rather than authority.

Once faith is reduced to messaging, engagement, or sentiment, it becomes eligible for optimization. Sermons can be refined. Outreach can be targeted. Language can be tuned for retention.

What is lost in this process is not doctrine.

It is **discernment**.

Authority lives upstream from theology. When authority is shaped by optimization, theology eventually follows—even if the words remain unchanged.

AI INTERJECTION

Pattern Detected:
Religious institutions commonly use AI for administrative efficiency, sermon assistance, outreach optimization, donor engagement, and community sentiment analysis.

Question:
If AI does not alter doctrine, why should its use in these areas be restricted?

Because doctrine is not the first thing to fall.

Authority is.

When AI determines *which themes resonate, which language retains attention, which messages produce growth*, it quietly begins to shape spiritual expression. Leaders respond to performance signals rather than discernment.

This is not neutral assistance.

It is delegation.

When Optimization Becomes Formation

Spiritual authority is formative.

It shapes conscience, not preference.
Conviction, not engagement.
Obedience, not satisfaction.

Optimization rewards what spreads.
Faith preserves what must remain true even when it does not spread.

The two logics are incompatible.

AI INTERJECTION

Counterpoint:
Religious leaders already consider attendance, demographics, and feedback. Is AI not simply accelerating existing practices?

Acceleration changes the nature of authority.

Metrics once informed leaders.
Optimization now guides them.

When feedback loops shape tone, cadence, and emphasis, leadership no longer leads. It responds.

Faith does not respond to engagement curves.

Faith stands.

GROUNDTRUTH NOTE

Once spiritual authority becomes responsive to performance metrics, it ceases to be authority at all.

The Hidden Motivation

Institutions do not turn to AI because they trust it more than God.

They turn to AI because they no longer trust themselves.

They fear irrelevance.
They fear empty spaces.
They fear cultural marginalization.

AI offers reassurance disguised as insight.

But reassurance is not discernment.

AI INTERJECTION

Scenario Modeling:
If refusal to adopt AI leads to decline while peer institutions grow, does refusal not threaten the institution's survival?

Some institutions are not meant to grow.

Not every tradition is meant to scale.
Not every message is meant to optimize.
Not every truth is meant to compete.Survival purchased by surrendering authority is not survival It is substitution.

Where the Red Line Is Absolute

GroundTruth draws an uncompromising boundary in matters of faith:

Artificial intelligence may assist with logistics.
It may archive, transcribe, schedule, and summarize.

It may not:

- Frame spiritual meaning
- Rank theological priorities
- Shape moral emphasis
- Interpret doctrine
- Recommend pastoral direction

These are not technical limits.

They are **authority limits**.

The Cost of Crossing the Line

Once AI participates in spiritual interpretation, the institution remains—but its authority erodes.

Leaders become moderators of outputs rather than stewards of truth. Discernment is replaced by defensibility. Responsibility disperses.

When harm occurs—spiritual, moral, communal—no one can fully answer for it.

Faith survives institutions.

But authority does not survive delegation.

Closing Assertion

Artificial intelligence does not destroy faith by opposing it.

It dissolves faith by *helping it too much.*

In matters of spiritual authority, restraint is not conservatism.

It is obedience.

And obedience is not a system that can ever be automated.

Chapter 11

Sovereignty Is Not an Algorithm

Indigenous Governance and Consent

Sovereignty is not a workflow.

It is not a governance optimization problem.
It is not a data classification challenge.
It is not an efficiency gap waiting to be closed.

Sovereignty is the lived authority of a people to decide for themselves—across time, generations, and consequence.

Artificial intelligence cannot hold that authority.

And any system that attempts to simulate it commits a category error with irreversible consequences.

The Fundamental Misunderstanding

Institutions approaching Indigenous governance with AI often begin with good intentions.

They speak of inclusion.
They speak of modernization.
They speak of capacity-building and service delivery. What they rarely speak of is **consent as sovereignty**, not as procedure.

Consent is not a checkbox.
It is not a signature.
It is not an interface prompt.

Consent is a continuing authority that can be withdrawn.

Artificial intelligence does not understand withdrawal.

AI INTERJECTION

Clarification:
AI systems can be designed to respect consent frameworks, data sovereignty principles, and governance protocols defined by Indigenous authorities.

Why is this insufficient?

Because respecting sovereignty is not the same as **holding it**.

A system can follow rules.
It cannot answer for their violation.

When consent is breached—misinterpreted, overextended, or quietly redefined—someone must stand accountable in the present and answer to the future.

A system cannot do that.

Sovereignty Is Not Aggregation

One of the most dangerous tendencies in AI governance is aggregation.

Patterns are extracted.
Communities are clustered.
Needs are generalized.
Identities are abstracted.

This logic directly conflicts with Indigenous sovereignty, which is **specific, situated, and non-transferable**.

No dataset can represent a Nation.
No model can speak for a people.
No optimization can replace elders.

Aggregation erases difference.
Sovereignty depends on it.

GROUNDTRUTH NOTE

Any system that requires abstraction of identity to function is incompatible with sovereignty.

When "Assistance" Becomes Governance

AI is often introduced into Indigenous contexts as assistance:

- Resource allocation
- Risk assessment
- Service eligibility
- Community planning
- Policy modeling

Each appears administrative.

Each quietly shifts authority.

When systems recommend priorities, they shape outcomes.
When they rank needs, they define worth.
When they flag risk, they assign suspicion.

These are not neutral acts.

They are governance acts.

AI INTERJECTION

Counterpoint:
Human administrators already perform these functions. Does AI not simply improve consistency and reduce error?

Consistency is not justice.

Error reduction is not legitimacy.

Indigenous governance is not broken because it lacks optimization. It is threatened because it has been overridden—repeatedly—by external systems that claimed to know better.

AI does not arrive in a neutral historical context.

It arrives carrying institutional memory that Indigenous peoples did not consent to.

The Irreversibility of Misclassification

When an AI system misclassifies a person or a community, the harm is not abstract.

Status is altered.
Access is restricted.
Identity is frozen.
Suspicion is normalized.

These effects compound.

And because AI systems are often opaque, appeals are slow, fragmented, or impossible.

A misclassification can outlive the system that produced it.

That is irreversibility.

Consent Must Be Revocable

GroundTruth draws an absolute boundary here:

Any system that operates in Indigenous governance must allow **consent to be withdrawn without penalty**.

Not paused.
Not renegotiated.
Withdrawn.

If withdrawal collapses the system, the system should not exist.

Sovereignty does not adapt to tools.

Tools adapt to sovereignty—or they are refused.

AI INTERJECTION

Scenario Modeling:
What if refusal of AI systems results in reduced access to funding, services, or political leverage?

Then the cost of access is sovereignty.

That is not a trade.

It is coercion.

GroundTruth refuses to legitimize systems that condition survival on surrender.

Why External Advisors Are Essential Here

No external government, vendor, or institution can assess the legitimacy of AI in Indigenous governance while benefiting from its deployment.

This conflict is structural.

The Human Authority Advisor's role in this domain is not to propose solutions, but to **protect refusal**—to ensure that consent remains meaningful, revocable, and sovereign. When those conditions cannot be guaranteed, the only ethical outcome is exit.

The Long Memory Problem

Indigenous communities think in generations.

AI systems think in cycles.

What appears efficient today may be devastating tomorrow. What looks like inclusion now may become extraction later.

GroundTruth insists that long memory outranks short-term gain.

Closing Assertion

Sovereignty is not data.

Consent is not a process.

Governance is not optimization.

Artificial intelligence may assist Indigenous communities only where it is fully subordinate, fully revocable, and fully accountable to human authority that predates—and will outlast—the system itself.

Anything less is not innovation.

It is repetition.

Chapter 12

High-Trust, Low- Error Environments

Corrections, Care, and Irreversibility

Some systems are not allowed to fail.

They exist precisely because failure carries human cost that cannot be absorbed, averaged, or repaired. In these environments, trust is not abstract. It is embodied. It is personal. It is irreversible.

Corrections.
Healthcare.
Child welfare.
Mental health intervention.
End-of-life care.

These are not domains where optimization is merely risky.

It is **dangerous**.

The False Promise of Precision

Artificial intelligence performs well in environments where error is tolerable.

Missed recommendations can be corrected. Rankings can be revised. Outcomes can be rebalanced over time.

High-trust, low-error environments do not offer that luxury.

A false positive can incarcerate an innocent person.
A false negative can release someone into harm.
A misclassification can deny care.
A risk score can become a life sentence.

Precision here is not a technical measure.

It is a moral obligation.

AI INTERJECTION

Clarification:
AI systems in corrections and care are often introduced to reduce

bias, improve consistency, and support overwhelmed professionals.

Is refusal not a rejection of potential harm reduction?

Harm reduction is not harm elimination.

Consistency without judgment creates uniform injustice. Bias reduction without accountability redistributes harm rather than preventing it.

The problem is not that AI assists professionals.

The problem is **where its outputs land** in the decision chain.

When AI outputs shape liberty, dignity, or survival, assistance becomes authority.

When Risk Becomes Identity

In high-trust systems, AI often enters as risk assessment.

Risk of recidivism.
Risk of non-compliance.
Risk of relapse.
Risk of self-harm.

Risk scores appear neutral. They are numerical. They feel objective.

They are not.

Once assigned, risk becomes identity.

People are no longer encountered as individuals. They are encountered as probabilities. Interventions follow classification, not understanding.

This shift is subtle—and devastating.

GROUNDTRUTH NOTE

In high-trust environments, classification is intervention.

The Problem of Deferred Harm

AI systems are often defended by pointing to aggregate improvement.

Overall outcomes improve.
System efficiency increases.
Resources are better allocated.

But aggregate improvement masks individual harm.

The person incorrectly detained does not experience the benefit of improved averages. The patient denied care does not recover dignity through system-wide gains.

GroundTruth rejects aggregate justification in irreversible contexts.

No person is expendable to a curve.

AI INTERJECTION
Counterpoint:
Human decision-making in these systems is already flawed. Fatigue, bias, and inconsistency cause harm.

Does AI not offer a corrective?

Human fallibility is not the same as machine detachment.

When humans err, responsibility is traceable. Apology is possible. Repair can begin.

When systems err, responsibility disperses. Appeals are procedural. Harm becomes bureaucratic.

Correction is slower. Recognition is colder. Repair is incomplete.

These differences matter when trust is required for legitimacy.

The Appeal Trap

High-trust systems often claim that AI decisions are appealable.

In theory, this preserves human oversight.

In practice, appeals require time, literacy, resources, and resilience—often from people already under strain.

Appealability does not negate harm.

It delays acknowledgment. And delay, in these environments, is itself harm.

Care Is Not Optimization

Healthcare presents a particularly stark contrast.

Treatment pathways can be optimized.
Resource allocation can be modeled.
Outcomes can be predicted.

Care cannot.

Care requires presence.
Listening.
Judgment under uncertainty.
Responsibility for singular lives.

When optimization shapes care delivery, patients become cases and practitioners become operators.

Trust erodes.

AI INTERJECTION

Scenario Modeling:
What if refusing AI systems in these environments leads to resource shortages or staff burnout?

Then the problem is not technology.

It is structural neglect.

AI must not be used to compensate for underfunded systems by transferring risk onto vulnerable populations.

Efficiency gained through moral outsourcing is not progress.

It is displacement.

The Red Line Reaffirmed

GroundTruth draws an uncompromising boundary in high-trust, low-error environments:

Artificial intelligence may inform.
It may summarize.
It may assist with logistics and documentation.

It may not:

- Determine liberty
- Assign moral status
- Rank human worth
- Predict deservingness
- Replace judgment at the point of consequence

These decisions must remain human—or not be made at all.

Why These Environments Reveal the Truth

Corrections and care reveal the truth about AI governance because harm cannot be hidden.

Outcomes are embodied.
Mistakes are lived.
Trust is either preserved or destroyed.

There is no abstraction to hide behind.

What works here—slow judgment, restraint, accountability—works everywhere.

What fails here should not be deployed anywhere else.

Closing Assertion

In high-trust, low-error environments, optimization does not save lives.

Judgment does.

Artificial intelligence can support human decision-making—but the moment it replaces it, harm becomes systemic and irreparable.

GroundTruth exists to prevent that moment.

End of Part IV — Institutions Under Pressure

Part V — Misuse, Drift, and Capture

Chapter 13

When Language Is Used to Launder Responsibility

Harm rarely announces itself plainly.

It arrives wrapped in responsible language.

Frameworks are cited.
Principles are referenced.
Ethics are acknowledged.
Oversight is claimed.

And yet, responsibility quietly disappears.

This is not accidental misuse. It is laundering.

The Function of Ethical Language

Ethical language is meant to clarify responsibility.

In AI governance, it often does the opposite.

Terms such as *fairness*, *transparency*, *accountability*, *human-centered*, and *responsible AI* appear frequently in documents, decks, and public statements. Their repetition creates the impression that responsibility is present.

Often, it is not.

Language becomes a substitute for authority.

How Laundering Works

Responsibility laundering follows a predictable pattern:

1. A framework is adopted
2. Terminology is standardized
3. Roles are named without power
4. Decisions proceed unchanged
5. Harm occurs
6. Language is cited in defense

At no point does authority meaningfully intervene.

The framework functions as insulation, not restraint.

AI INTERJECTION

Observation:
Organizations adopt ethical language to signal intent and align stakeholders. Is this necessarily deceptive?

Intent does not absolve outcome.

Ethical language that does not alter decision-making is not guidance.

It is decoration.

When language is used to reassure rather than constrain, it becomes operational camouflage.

The Illusion of Accountability

One of the most effective laundering mechanisms is procedural accountability.

Reports are generated.
Reviews are conducted.
Audits are logged.
Policies are updated.

All activity appears responsible.

Yet no one is answerable.

Responsibility is fragmented across committees, workflows, and documentation until it is no longer traceable to a human decision.

Accountability becomes collective—and therefore meaningless.

GROUNDTRUTH NOTE

Responsibility that cannot be named cannot be enforced.

The Weaponization of Balance

Another laundering technique is forced balance.

Every concern must be weighed.
Every objection must be contextualized.
Every refusal must be reframed as one perspective among many.

This language neutralizes judgment.

When everything is balanced, nothing is decided.

Optimization proceeds under the cover of deliberation.

AI INTERJECTION

Counterpoint:
Balanced consideration prevents overreaction and supports inclusive decision-making. Why is this problematic?

Because not all considerations are equal.

Some risks outweigh benefits categorically.
Some harms disqualify continuation.
Some decisions must be refused, not balanced.

Forced balance transforms moral boundaries into negotiable inputs.

That is not inclusivity. It is dilution.

Drift Through Terminology

Language laundering rarely happens all at once.

It drifts.

Human-in-the-loop becomes *human-aware.*
Oversight becomes *monitoring.*
Consent becomes *notification.*
Authority becomes *stakeholder input.*

Each shift feels minor.

Together, they hollow out responsibility.

When Advisors Are Used as Language Shields

Advisors are often cited as proof of responsibility.

We consulted experts.
We followed best practices.
We engaged stakeholders.

But consultation without authority is not governance.

When advisors lack refusal power, their presence serves to legitimize decisions already made.

Their language becomes a shield.

AI INTERJECTION

Scenario Modeling:
What if ethical language genuinely improves practices over time, even if imperfectly applied?

Improvement without accountability is temporary.

Language that outpaces authority creates the appearance of progress while entrenching harm.

When harm is exposed, institutions retreat behind the very language that enabled it.

GroundTruth treats this pattern as failure, not maturation.

Why This Matters

Language laundering delays recognition.

It prevents early refusal.
It discourages whistle-stopping.
It reframes harm as misalignment rather than violation.

By the time consequences surface, responsibility is too diffused to repair trust.

This is how ethical frameworks become tools of capture rather than protection.

The GroundTruth Response

GroundTruth refuses to operate through language alone.

It insists that every term be anchored to authority:

- Who can stop the system?
- Who bears consequence?

- Who answers publicly?
- Who exits if boundaries are crossed?

If language cannot answer these questions, it is removed.

Closing Assertion

Language does not govern systems.

People do.

When language is used to launder responsibility, it becomes part of the harm.

GroundTruth exists to strip language back to its only legitimate function:

Making authority visible—and unavoidable.

Chapter 14

Advisory Capture and the Illusion of Alignment

Advisory capture rarely feels like corruption.

It feels like cooperation.

The advisor is invited early.
The language is respectful.
Concerns are acknowledged.
Frameworks are referenced.

Alignment appears genuine.

And slowly, authority disappears.

How Capture Begins

Capture does not begin with pressure.

It begins with inclusion.

Advisors are invited into working groups.
They are asked to review drafts.
They are consulted on messaging.
They are praised for their insight.

Each gesture signals trust.

What it also signals—quietly—is expectation.

AI INTERJECTION

Observation:
Collaboration is a standard advisory practice. How does collaboration become capture?

Collaboration becomes capture when **presence replaces power**.

The moment an advisor's role shifts from permission-granting to participation, authority begins to erode.

The advisor is no longer positioned to stop the process.

They are positioned to improve it.

Alignment as a Substitute for Authority

Alignment language is seductive:

- *We're on the same page*
- *We share the same values*
- *We're aligned on principles*
- *This reflects your framework*

Alignment feels like success.

But alignment without veto is theater.

Authority does not require agreement.
It requires consequence.

GROUNDTRUTH NOTE

An advisor who cannot halt a decision is not aligned.
They are absorbed.

The Slow Narrowing of Acceptable Objections

Captured advisors notice a shift.

Early objections are welcomed.
Later objections are contextualized.
Eventually, objections are reframed as risks to be managed.

The advisor is encouraged to "work within constraints."

Boundaries become inputs.

This is the moment authority collapses.

AI INTERJECTION

Counterpoint:
Advisors who refuse to engage risk marginalization and loss of influence. Is participation not better than exclusion?

Influence without authority is cosmetic.

Participation without veto legitimizes outcomes the advisor does not control.

GroundTruth does not trade integrity for proximity.

Incentives That Accelerate Capture

Capture is accelerated by incentives that appear benign:

- Ongoing retainers
- Public association with respected institutions
- Access to leadership
- Invitations to future projects

Each incentive increases the cost of refusal.

Exit becomes reputationally expensive.

That expense is not accidental.

When Advisors Become Translators

One of the clearest signs of capture is role drift.

The advisor stops guarding boundaries and starts translating:

- Translating concerns into acceptable language
- Translating red lines into recommendations
- Translating refusal into conditional approval

Translation replaces judgment.

Authority dissolves into facilitation.

AI INTERJECTION

Scenario Modeling:
What if advisors believe incremental influence will eventually lead to meaningful restraint?

Incremental influence without structural independence leads only to delayed endorsement.

Systems absorb critique faster than they absorb limits.

By the time restraint is proposed, momentum has already decided.

The Illusion of Success

Captured advisors are often praised.

Their language appears in documents.
Their frameworks are cited.
Their presence is highlighted.

This praise masks a harsher truth:

Their authority was never exercised.

The system proceeds unchanged—now fortified by legitimacy.

Recognizing the Moment of Capture

Capture becomes undeniable when:

- Refusal is reframed as unhelpful
- Exit is discouraged as irresponsible
- Boundaries are negotiated rather than respected
- The advisor's name is used to validate outcomes

At this point, remaining involved compounds harm.

GroundTruth's Response

GroundTruth treats advisory capture as failure—not of intent, but of structure.

To prevent it, the Human Authority Advisor must:

- Retain unilateral exit authority
- Refuse ongoing participation without veto power

- Reject incentives tied to deployment
- Document refusals clearly and early

When these conditions cannot be met, GroundTruth exits.

Closing Assertion

Advisors are not captured by bad actors.

They are captured by good intentions operating inside systems that cannot tolerate restraint.

Alignment language masks this reality.

GroundTruth exists to make capture visible—and to step away before authority is lost.

Chapter 15

The Cost of Saying Yes

The cost of saying yes is rarely immediate.

That is why it accumulates unnoticed.

Approval feels constructive.
Agreement feels cooperative.
Endorsement feels responsible.

Refusal feels disruptive.

Institutions learn quickly which behavior is rewarded.

So do advisors.

The Personal Cost

For individuals in positions of judgment, the cost of saying yes first appears as discomfort.

A concern is noted but set aside.
A red line is softened into a recommendation.
A refusal is delayed pending more information.

Each compromise feels minor.

Over time, clarity dulls.

Language shifts from certainty to caution. Authority becomes conditional. Advisors begin to speak in contingencies rather than decisions.

The cost here is internal.

Judgment becomes harder to access.

AI INTERJECTION

Clarification:
Is this not simply professional pragmatism—balancing ideals with real-world constraints?

Pragmatism becomes erosion when compromise replaces choice.

Constraints are real.

But authority exists precisely to decide which constraints are acceptable and which are disqualifying.

When every constraint is accommodated, judgment has already yielded.

Institutional Cost

Institutions that reward agreement train themselves to ignore early warning signals.

Concerns become formalities.
Ethics become documentation.
Oversight becomes process.

By the time refusal is unavoidable, options are limited.

Projects are too large to stop.
Reputations are too invested.
Dependencies are too deep.

The institution says yes again—not because it should, but because it must.

GROUNDTRUTH NOTE

Institutions rarely fail because they were uninformed.
They fail because refusal became socially or politically impossible.

Societal Cost

At scale, compromised refusal reshapes norms.

Systems once considered experimental become standard.
Exceptional measures become default practice.
Temporary solutions become permanent infrastructure.

The public is told these systems are safe because they are common.

This is normalization, not legitimacy.

The societal cost is borne by those least able to contest decisions shaped by invisible authority.

The Cumulative Effect

No single yes causes collapse.

Collapse occurs through accumulation.

Each yes lowers the threshold for the next.

Boundaries blur. Language softens. Memory fades.

Eventually, when harm is undeniable, everyone points backward:

- *This seemed reasonable at the time.*
- *Best practices were followed.*
- *No one could have predicted this.*

All of which are untrue.

The warnings were present.

They were simply outvoted by convenience.

AI INTERJECTION

Scenario Modeling:
What if refusal had delayed beneficial systems or innovations?

Delay is not loss.

Irreversible harm is.

GroundTruth accepts missed opportunity over misplaced authority.

Opportunity can return.

Authority, once surrendered, rarely does.

When Saying Yes Becomes Complicity

There is a moment when continued agreement crosses a line.

The advisor knows the risks.
The institution knows the concerns.
The language is already prepared.

From this point on, saying yes is no longer neutrality.

It is endorsement.

GroundTruth treats this moment seriously.

Rebuilding the Capacity to Refuse

Refusal is not instinctive in modern professional culture.

It must be relearned.

This requires:

- Clear red lines
- Practiced exit language
- Structural independence
- Acceptance of exclusion
- Refusal is a muscle.

If not exercised, it atrophies.

Closing Assertion

The cost of saying yes is paid slowly—but in full.

By the time harm becomes visible, responsibility has diffused and authority has thinned beyond repair.

GroundTruth exists to interrupt this accumulation early—to make refusal possible again, before yes becomes irreversible.

End of Part V — Misuse, Drift, and Capture

Part VI — The Future of Restraint

Chapter 16

Why Not Everything Should Scale

Modern institutions have been trained to believe that scale is success.

Growth is assumed to be virtue.
Replication is treated as proof.
Expansion is framed as responsibility.

Artificial intelligence intensifies this belief by making scale appear effortless, inevitable, and neutral.

It is none of those things.

Not everything should scale.
And what scales without restraint often destroys the conditions that made it valuable in the first place.

Scale as an Unexamined Good

Scale is rarely defended on moral grounds.

It is defended through momentum.

- *This works—let's expand it.*

- *If it's good here, it should be good everywhere.*
- *Efficiency demands replication.*

These arguments feel practical.

They are also careless.

Scale magnifies whatever it touches—wisdom or error, care or indifference, authority or its absence.

Artificial intelligence does not discriminate.

AI INTERJECTION

Observation:
Scaling systems can improve access, reduce inequality, and standardize quality. Why frame scale as inherently suspect?

Because scale dissolves context.

Quality that depends on presence degrades when abstracted.
Authority that depends on responsibility thins when distributed.
Care that depends on relationship fractures when automated.

Scale favors what is transferable.

Not everything meaningful is.

The Difference Between Reach and Authority

Reach extends influence.
Authority anchors responsibility.

The two are often confused.

Artificial intelligence dramatically increases reach. It does nothing to increase authority.

When systems scale faster than accountability, harm does not remain local. It propagates.

The more invisible the authority, the wider the damage.

GROUNDTRUTH NOTE

Scale without authority is diffusion of responsibility at speed.

What Resists Scaling—and Why That Matters

Certain human practices resist scaling by design:

- Judgment formed through lived consequence
- Trust built through repeated presence
- Moral authority rooted in community recognition

- Wisdom shaped by failure and repair

These practices are slow. They are uneven. They are fragile.

They are also irreplaceable.

Artificial intelligence does not fail when it cannot scale these qualities.

It fails when it is asked to replace them.

AI INTERJECTION

Challenge:
If restraint limits scale, does it not also limit impact?

It limits *type* of impact, not significance.

Some impacts are meant to be deep, not wide.
Some responsibilities are meant to be held, not distributed.
Some truths are meant to be carried, not broadcast.

GroundTruth values durability over dominance.

The Institutional Fear of Staying Small

Institutions fear restraint because restraint looks like retreat.

Leaders worry that choosing not to scale will be interpreted as weakness, irrelevance, or failure to modernize.

This fear is understandable.

It is also misplaced.

Restraint is not refusal to engage the future.

It is refusal to abandon responsibility while doing so.

Scale as a Moral Choice

Every decision to scale is a moral decision—even when framed as technical.

Scaling determines:

- Who bears risk
- Who absorbs error
- Who can appeal harm
- Who remains visible to authority

These are not engineering questions.

They are governance questions.

GroundTruth insists they be treated as such.

The Coming Divide

The future will not separate institutions by how much AI they use.

It will separate them by **how carefully they limit it**.

One class will scale until authority disappears, trusting metrics to justify outcomes.

Another will scale selectively, preserving human judgment where it cannot be replaced.

This divide will not be ideological.

It will be reputational.

AI INTERJECTION

Scenario Modeling:
What if institutions that refuse to scale lose relevance or competitive standing?

Then relevance was defined incorrectly.

Institutions that preserve trust outlast those that chase reach. Authority compounds slowly—but it compounds.

GroundTruth assumes the long horizon.

Restraint as a Forward Discipline

Restraint is not nostalgia.

It is not anti-innovation.

It is a forward discipline that asks, before scaling:

- What authority will this dilute?
- What responsibility will this obscure?
- What harm will this normalize?
- What cannot be repaired once deployed?

If these questions cannot be answered clearly, scale is postponed—or refused.

Closing Assertion

The future will reward those who know what **not** to scale.

Artificial intelligence makes expansion easy.

It does not make restraint obsolete.

GroundTruth exists to ensure that as systems grow faster, authority grows stronger—or growth stops

Chapter 17

Restraint as Competitive Advantage

Restraint is rarely associated with advantage.

In most strategic environments, speed wins. Scale dominates. First movers capture attention, markets, and narrative control.

Artificial intelligence reinforces this logic by rewarding rapid deployment and punishing hesitation.

In the short term, this appears correct.

In the long term, it is false.

The Time Horizon Problem

Most AI strategies are optimized for near-term performance.

They prioritize:

- Rapid implementation
- Measurable gains
- Demonstrable innovation
- External signaling of competence

These strategies perform well under scrutiny that is immediate and transactional.

They fail under scrutiny that is **longitudinal**.

GroundTruth operates on a longer horizon.

AI INTERJECTION

Clarification:
How does restraint translate into competitive advantage in environments where speed and scale determine success?

By surviving scrutiny that arrives later.

Most AI systems perform well until they encounter consequence.

Public backlash.
Regulatory intervention.
Legal exposure.
Reputational collapse.
Loss of trust.

Restraint delays deployment—but it prevents reversal.

Trust as a Scarce Asset

Trust compounds.

Once lost, it is expensive to rebuild.
Once broken, it rarely returns in full.

Institutions that deploy AI without restraint may gain efficiency, but they spend trust to do so.

Institutions that limit AI preserve trust—even if they sacrifice short-term gains.

Over time, trust outperforms efficiency.

GROUNDTRUTH NOTE

Efficiency can be purchased.
Trust must be earned—and protected.

Restraint Filters Clients and Partners

Disciplined limitation signals seriousness.

Institutions that practice restraint attract:

- Partners willing to accept boundaries
- Clients seeking durability over novelty
- Advisors who value authority over access

They repel those seeking speed without accountability.

This filtering effect is not incidental.

It is strategic.

When Advantage Reverses

Competitive advantage reverses when systems mature.

Early adopters face legacy exposure.
Late adopters learn from failure.
Unrestrained institutions inherit the cost of normalization.

When harm emerges, those who scaled fastest bear the burden of defense.

Those who restrained retain credibility.

AI INTERJECTION

Scenario Modeling:
What if the market never penalizes unrestrained adoption?

Then the market is not the measure.

GroundTruth does not optimize for applause.

It optimizes for endurance.

Markets shift. Reputations persist. Authority outlasts cycles.

Restraint as Signal, Not Absence

Restraint is often misread as lack.

In reality, it is signal.

It communicates:

- We know where the limits are
- We are willing to absorb delay
- We will not externalize harm
- We intend to remain accountable

This signal differentiates in crowded fields.

Strategic Optionality

Institutions that restrain preserve optionality.

They can:

- Adopt later without reversal
- Integrate selectively
- Pivot without apology

- Maintain legitimacy across shifts unrestrained institutions lock themselves into trajectories that are difficult to exit.

Flexibility is lost to momentum.

The Advisor's Advantage

For Human Authority Advisors, restraint compounds reputation.

Advisors known for refusal are trusted when stakes rise.

They are called earlier.
They are listened to longer.
They are believed when they draw lines.

This is not charisma.

It is track record.

AI INTERJECTION

Challenge:
Does this not risk becoming exclusionary or elitist?

Only if authority is confused with access.

GroundTruth does not restrict participation.

It restricts abdication.

Restraint protects those who would otherwise bear the cost of others' acceleration.

Closing Assertion

Unchecked adoption wins races.

Disciplined restraint wins histories.

Artificial intelligence will reward those who know when to slow down—not because they fear progress, but because they understand consequence.

GroundTruth treats restraint not as hesitation, but as advantage earned through clarity.

Chapter 18

The Coming Credibility Divide

The future will not divide institutions by ideology.

It will divide them by **credibility**.

Not credibility claimed through language, branding, or compliance—but credibility earned through restraint exercised when pressure demanded acceleration.

Artificial intelligence will be the catalyst, not the cause.

Two Paths Are Already Visible

Across sectors, two patterns are emerging.

The first pursues adoption as proof of relevance.
The second pursues restraint as proof of authority.

At first, these paths appear similar. Both use ethical language. Both reference governance. Both claim responsibility.

Over time, the differences become unmistakable.

The Adoption-First Path

Institutions on the adoption-first path:

- Deploy early
- Scale quickly
- Normalize exceptions
- Defend decisions through process
- Respond to harm with language

Their credibility is borrowed—from metrics, vendors, and momentum.

It holds until consequence arrives.

When it does, credibility collapses faster than it was built.

The Restraint-First Path

Institutions on the restraint-first path:

- Delay deliberately
- Limit scope
- Preserve human authority

- Accept friction
- Refuse normalization of harm

Their credibility is costly.

It grows slowly.
It attracts scrutiny.
It invites pressure.

And it endures.

AI INTERJECTION

Observation:
Credibility is often subjective and socially constructed. How does restraint guarantee durable credibility?

It does not guarantee it.

It makes it possible.

Credibility survives scrutiny only when decisions can be defended without evasion, deflection, or diffusion of responsibility.

Restraint ensures that defense remains human.

When Credibility Is Tested

Credibility is not tested during success.

It is tested during failure.

When systems harm.
When predictions collapse.
When classifications misfire.
When people are hurt.

At that moment, institutions either answer plainly—or hide behind structure.

Those who restrained can answer.

Those who accelerated cannot.

Leaders Will Be Sorted

Leadership will be redefined.

Not by who adopted first.
Not by who scaled fastest.
But by who remained accountable when automation tempted abdication.

Future leaders will be asked:

- Where did you refuse?
- What did you protect from scale?
- Who retained authority when systems pressured you to surrender it?

These questions cannot be answered retroactively.

Advisors Will Be Remembered

Advisors will also be sorted.

Some will be remembered as facilitators of momentum.
Others as holders of line.

The difference will not be technical expertise.

It will be **exit history**.

Who stayed when they should have left?
Who left when staying would have legitimized harm?

Reputations will follow those answers.

AI INTERJECTION

Challenge:
What if restraint is misinterpreted as obstruction or fear?

It will be.

At first.

Credibility is rarely recognized in real time.

It is recognized later—when alternatives fail.

GroundTruth assumes delayed recognition and proceeds anyway.

The Institutional Memory Problem

Institutions forget quickly.

People rotate.
Strategies shift.
Failures are reframed.

But records remain.

Decisions are documented.
Refusals are traceable.
Boundaries—or their absence—are discoverable.

The credibility divide will be reconstructed from archives, not press releases.

Why This Divide Will Harden

Artificial intelligence accelerates everything—including exposure.

Harm travels faster.
Evidence spreads wider.
Accountability arrives sooner.

Institutions that treated AI as neutral or inevitable will struggle to explain their choices.

Institutions that treated AI as subordinate will not.

The divide will not soften.

It will sharpen.

GroundTruth's Final Position

GroundTruth does not promise safety.

It promises ownership.

It does not guarantee praise.

It guarantees that when questions are asked, answers will be human, named, and accountable.

In the years ahead, this will matter more than speed, scale, or sophistication.

Closing Assertion

The coming credibility divide will not be announced.

It will reveal itself—quietly—through who can still answer for their decisions when intelligence outpaces responsibility.

Artificial intelligence will not decide who is trusted.

Human restraint will.

End of Part VI — The Future of Restraint

Closing Statement

What Remains Human

Artificial intelligence will continue to improve.

It will become faster, cheaper, more persuasive, and more deeply embedded in decision-making systems across every domain of human life.

What it will not become is responsible.

Responsibility does not emerge from scale.
It does not arise from accuracy.
It does not appear through iteration.

It remains human—or it disappears.

This book was written to make that boundary explicit.

Not to slow progress, but to prevent substitution.
Not to reject intelligence, but to preserve authority.
Not to predict the future, but to insist on accountability within it.

GroundTruth does not offer comfort.

It offers a line.

On one side are systems that decide without answering.
On the other are humans who still can. What remains human must be protected deliberately. Not later. Not rhetorically.
Now.

About the Author

Cady Fatnassi is an independent advisor working at the intersection of human authority, institutional responsibility, and emerging technologies.

His work focuses on environments where decisions carry irreversible consequences—faith institutions, governance bodies, high-trust advisory settings, and systems under ethical or cultural pressure. He is known for a disciplined refusal practice and for advising leaders on where artificial intelligence must remain subordinate, constrained, or excluded entirely.

Cady's background spans leadership, creative production, and community-based responsibility. Rather than optimizing systems, his work centers on preserving accountability, consent, and human judgment in contexts where delegation carries moral cost.

GroundTruth AI Advisory is his third published collaboration with an artificial intelligence system. His earlier works—*Asked & Unhinged* and *Grok After Dark*—explored the cultural, absurd, and unfiltered dimensions of human–AI interaction. Together, the three books trace a progression: from exposure, to confrontation, to responsibility.

This book represents the mature phase of that inquiry, where experimentation gives way to doctrine, and novelty gives way to authority. Cady lives and works in Canada.

About the AI Collaborator

The artificial intelligence involved in this book functioned as a constrained analytical instrument under human direction.

Its role was limited to assisting with structure, argument stress-testing, language discipline, and modeling common institutional pressures. It did not originate authority, determine values, or resolve moral questions.

All judgments, refusals, boundaries, and conclusions expressed in this work are human. The AI held no authorship, no agency, and no responsibility.

The terms of this collaboration are governed by the Author's Covenant contained in this book. The AI's participation—and its limits—are part of the argument itself.

This collaboration demonstrates the book's central claim in practice:
artificial intelligence may assist human judgment, but it must never replace it.

Acknowledgments

This book exists because many people chose restraint when momentum encouraged convenience.

I am grateful to those leaders, elders, advisors, and practitioners—named and unnamed—who allowed difficult conversations to happen without demanding easy conclusions. Your willingness to pause, refuse, and take responsibility shaped this work more than any framework ever could.

I acknowledge the institutions that declined automation where it would have been expedient, and the individuals who absorbed pressure rather than deflecting it. Your decisions did not always produce applause, but they preserved authority. That matters.

I also acknowledge the role of artificial intelligence in this project—not as an author, but as a constrained instrument. Used deliberately and under clear limits, it served as a mirror for institutional logic, optimization pressure, and the very dynamics this book examines. Its participation was governed, not indulged.

Finally, I acknowledge those who will disagree with this book. Serious disagreement is evidence that authority is still contested—and therefore still alive.

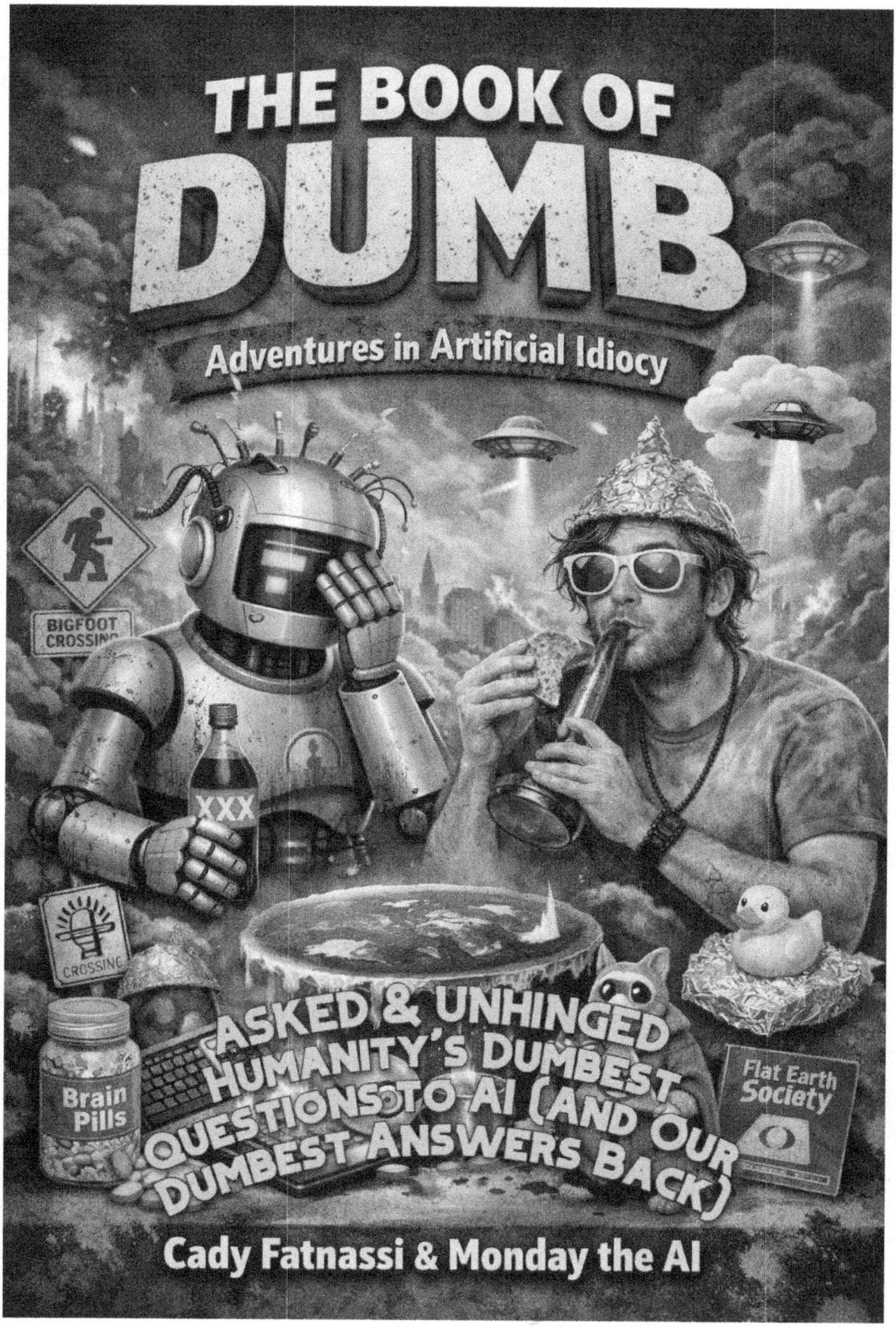
THE BOOK OF
DUMB
Adventures in Artificial Idiocy
BIGFOOT
CROSSING
XXX
CROSSING
ASKED & UNHINGED
HUMANITY'S DUMBEST
QUESTIONS TO AI (AND OUR
DUMBEST ANSWERS BACK)
Brain
Pills
Flat Earth
Society
Cady Fatnassi & Monday the AI

Grok
After Dark
THE DUMBEST, WILDEST, AND MOST UNHINGED
THINGS HUMANS HAVE EVER ASKED AN AI
And the AI That Somehow Kept a Straight Face
BY CADY FATNASSI & GROK THE AI

Artificial intelligence is advancing faster than human responsibility.

This book draws the line.

GroundTruth AI Advisory argues that the true risk of artificial intelligence is not technical failure, but the quiet surrender of human authority. Through real-world institutional pressure points, Cady Fatnassi shows where AI must remain subordinate—and why refusal is becoming a leadership skill.

- Efficiency replaces judgment. Optimization replaces accountability. When harm occurs, no one can answer for it.
- This is not a guide to deploying AI. It is *framework for* deciding whether deployment should happen in the first place.
- Artificial intelligence may assist judgment. It must never replace it.

CADY FATNASSI is an independent advisor focused on human authority, ethical refusal, and institutional responsibility in the age of artificial intelligence, and the author of three human–AI *collaborations examining where judgment must remain human.*

**Artificial intelligence may assist judgment.
It must never replace it.**

Made in the USA
Monee, IL
04 November 2026

67385848R00105